50 Premium Dinner Roll Recipes

By: Kelly Johnson

Table of Contents

- Classic Parker House Rolls
- Garlic Herb Butter Rolls
- Honey Butter Dinner Rolls
- Brioche Dinner Rolls
- Whole Wheat Rolls
- Potato Dinner Rolls
- Milk Bread Rolls
- Buttermilk Rolls
- Sourdough Dinner Rolls
- Hawaiian Sweet Rolls
- Parmesan Herb Rolls
- Cheddar Garlic Rolls
- Rosemary Sea Salt Rolls
- Soft Pretzel Rolls
- Sweet Cornbread Rolls
- Sesame Seed Rolls
- Poppy Seed Rolls
- Cinnamon Honey Rolls
- Cheddar Jalapeño Rolls
- Olive Oil and Herb Rolls
- Maple Butter Rolls
- Rye Dinner Rolls
- Multigrain Rolls
- Sun-Dried Tomato Basil Rolls
- Asiago Cheese Rolls
- Dill and Cheddar Rolls
- Caramelized Onion Rolls
- Lemon Thyme Rolls
- Spelt Flour Rolls
- Crusty French Rolls
- Pumpkin Spice Rolls
- Orange Honey Butter Rolls
- Cranberry Walnut Rolls
- Bacon and Cheddar Rolls
- Herb and Garlic Knots

- Ricotta Rolls
- Black Pepper and Parmesan Rolls
- Cinnamon Raisin Rolls
- Spinach and Feta Rolls
- Sweet Potato Rolls
- Yeast-Free Dinner Rolls
- Vegan Herb Rolls
- Gluten-Free Dinner Rolls
- Chive and Sour Cream Rolls
- Molasses Wheat Rolls
- Buttery Crescent Rolls
- Pesto Swirl Rolls
- Lemon Poppy Seed Rolls
- Flaky Butter Layer Rolls
- Almond Milk Dinner Rolls

Classic Parker House Rolls

Ingredients:

- 4 cups (480g) all-purpose flour
- 1/3 cup (65g) granulated sugar
- 2 teaspoons salt
- 1 packet (2 and 1/4 tsp) active dry yeast
- 1/2 cup (120ml) warm milk
- 1/2 cup (120ml) warm water
- 1/3 cup (75g) unsalted butter, melted
- 1 large egg

Instructions:

1. **Activate yeast**: Mix warm milk, water, and yeast. Let sit for 5 minutes until foamy.
2. **Mix dough**: In a large bowl, combine flour, sugar, salt, butter, egg, and yeast mixture. Knead until smooth.
3. **First rise**: Cover and let rise for 1 hour or until doubled in size.
4. **Shape rolls**: Roll dough into a rectangle, cut into squares, and fold in half. Arrange on a baking sheet.
5. **Second rise**: Let rise for 30 minutes.
6. **Bake**: Brush with melted butter and bake at 375°F (190°C) for 15-20 minutes.

Garlic Herb Butter Rolls

Ingredients:

- 4 cups (480g) all-purpose flour
- 1/4 cup (50g) sugar
- 1 and 1/2 teaspoons salt
- 1 packet (2 and 1/4 tsp) instant yeast
- 1/4 cup (60ml) olive oil
- 1 cup (240ml) warm water
- 1 teaspoon garlic powder
- 2 tablespoons chopped fresh herbs (parsley, rosemary, thyme)

Instructions:

1. **Prepare dough**: Combine flour, sugar, salt, yeast, garlic powder, and herbs. Add warm water and olive oil. Knead until smooth.
2. **First rise**: Cover and let rise for 1 hour.
3. **Shape rolls**: Divide into balls and place on a greased baking sheet.
4. **Second rise**: Let rise for 30 minutes.
5. **Bake**: Brush with herb butter and bake at 375°F (190°C) for 15-20 minutes.

Honey Butter Dinner Rolls

Ingredients:

- 3 and 1/2 cups (420g) all-purpose flour
- 1/4 cup (60ml) honey
- 1 teaspoon salt
- 1 packet (2 and 1/4 tsp) instant yeast
- 1/2 cup (120ml) warm milk
- 1/4 cup (60g) unsalted butter, melted
- 1 large egg

Instructions:

1. **Mix dough**: Combine flour, yeast, salt, honey, milk, butter, and egg. Knead until soft.
2. **First rise**: Cover and let rise for 1 hour.
3. **Shape rolls**: Form dough into balls and arrange in a greased baking dish.
4. **Second rise**: Let rise for 30 minutes.
5. **Bake**: Brush with honey butter and bake at 375°F (190°C) for 18-20 minutes.

Brioche Dinner Rolls

Ingredients:

- 3 and 3/4 cups (450g) all-purpose flour
- 1/4 cup (50g) sugar
- 1 teaspoon salt
- 1 packet (2 and 1/4 tsp) instant yeast
- 1/2 cup (120ml) warm milk
- 3 large eggs
- 1/2 cup (120g) unsalted butter, softened

Instructions:

1. **Mix dough**: Combine flour, sugar, salt, yeast, milk, and eggs. Knead in butter until smooth.
2. **First rise**: Cover and let rise for 1-2 hours.
3. **Shape rolls**: Divide dough into balls and place in a greased pan.
4. **Second rise**: Let rise for 1 hour.
5. **Bake**: Brush with egg wash and bake at 375°F (190°C) for 20-25 minutes.

Whole Wheat Rolls

Ingredients:

- 2 cups (240g) whole wheat flour
- 1 and 1/2 cups (180g) all-purpose flour
- 1/4 cup (50g) sugar
- 1 teaspoon salt
- 1 packet (2 and 1/4 tsp) instant yeast
- 1 cup (240ml) warm milk
- 1/4 cup (60ml) vegetable oil

Instructions:

1. **Combine ingredients**: Mix flours, sugar, salt, yeast, milk, and oil. Knead until smooth.
2. **First rise**: Cover and let rise for 1 hour.
3. **Shape rolls**: Form into balls and arrange in a greased dish.
4. **Second rise**: Let rise for 30 minutes.
5. **Bake**: Bake at 375°F (190°C) for 15-18 minutes.

Potato Dinner Rolls

Ingredients:

- 1 cup (240g) mashed potatoes
- 3 cups (360g) all-purpose flour
- 1/4 cup (50g) sugar
- 1 teaspoon salt
- 1 packet (2 and 1/4 tsp) instant yeast
- 1/4 cup (60ml) warm milk
- 1/4 cup (60g) unsalted butter, melted

Instructions:

1. **Mix dough**: Combine flour, sugar, salt, yeast, mashed potatoes, milk, and butter. Knead until soft.
2. **First rise**: Let rise for 1 hour.
3. **Shape rolls**: Form into balls and place on a greased baking sheet.
4. **Second rise**: Let rise for 30 minutes.
5. **Bake**: Bake at 375°F (190°C) for 15-20 minutes.

Milk Bread Rolls

Ingredients:

- 2 and 1/2 cups (300g) all-purpose flour
- 1/4 cup (50g) sugar
- 1 teaspoon salt
- 1/2 cup (120ml) warm milk
- 1/4 cup (60ml) heavy cream
- 1 egg
- 1/4 cup (60g) unsalted butter, softened
- 1 teaspoon yeast

Instructions:

1. **Prepare dough**: Mix flour, sugar, salt, milk, cream, egg, butter, and yeast. Knead until smooth.
2. **First rise**: Let rise for 1 hour.
3. **Shape rolls**: Divide dough into portions and shape.
4. **Second rise**: Let rise for 30 minutes.
5. **Bake**: Bake at 350°F (175°C) for 15-18 minutes.

Buttermilk Rolls

Ingredients:

- 3 cups (360g) all-purpose flour
- 1/4 cup (50g) sugar
- 1 teaspoon salt
- 1 packet (2 and 1/4 tsp) instant yeast
- 1/2 cup (120ml) buttermilk
- 1/4 cup (60g) unsalted butter, melted

Instructions:

1. **Mix dough**: Combine flour, sugar, salt, yeast, buttermilk, and butter. Knead until smooth.
2. **First rise**: Cover and let rise for 1 hour.
3. **Shape rolls**: Form into balls and place in a greased pan.
4. **Second rise**: Let rise for 30 minutes.
5. **Bake**: Bake at 375°F (190°C) for 18-20 minutes.

Sourdough Dinner Rolls

Ingredients:

- 1 cup (240g) active sourdough starter
- 3 cups (360g) all-purpose flour
- 1 tablespoon sugar
- 1 teaspoon salt
- 1/4 cup (60ml) warm water
- 1/4 cup (60g) unsalted butter, softened

Instructions:

1. **Mix dough**: Combine starter, flour, sugar, salt, water, and butter. Knead until smooth.
2. **First rise**: Let rise for 4-6 hours at room temperature.
3. **Shape rolls**: Form into balls and place on a greased tray.
4. **Second rise**: Let rise for 1-2 hours.
5. **Bake**: Bake at 375°F (190°C) for 20-25 minutes.

Hawaiian Sweet Rolls

Ingredients:

- 4 cups (480g) all-purpose flour
- 1/4 cup (60ml) pineapple juice
- 1/4 cup (60g) sugar
- 1/4 cup (60g) unsalted butter, melted
- 1/4 cup (60ml) milk
- 1 large egg
- 2 teaspoons salt
- 1 packet (2 and 1/4 tsp) instant yeast

Instructions:

1. **Prepare dough**: Combine flour, sugar, salt, yeast, pineapple juice, milk, egg, and butter. Knead until soft.
2. **First rise**: Cover and let rise for 1-2 hours.
3. **Shape rolls**: Divide into balls and arrange in a greased baking dish.
4. **Second rise**: Let rise for 30 minutes.
5. **Bake**: Bake at 375°F (190°C) for 15-20 minutes.

Parmesan Herb Rolls

Ingredients:

- 4 cups (480g) all-purpose flour
- 1/4 cup (50g) grated Parmesan cheese
- 1 teaspoon dried oregano
- 1 teaspoon dried basil
- 1 teaspoon salt
- 1 packet (2 and 1/4 tsp) instant yeast
- 1/4 cup (60ml) olive oil
- 1 cup (240ml) warm water

Instructions:

1. **Combine ingredients**: Mix flour, Parmesan, herbs, salt, yeast, water, and olive oil. Knead until smooth.
2. **First rise**: Cover and let rise for 1 hour.
3. **Shape rolls**: Form dough into balls and place on a baking sheet.
4. **Second rise**: Let rise for 30 minutes.
5. **Bake**: Bake at 375°F (190°C) for 15-18 minutes.

Cheddar Garlic Rolls

Ingredients:

- 4 cups (480g) all-purpose flour
- 1 and 1/2 cups (150g) shredded cheddar cheese
- 1 teaspoon garlic powder
- 1 teaspoon salt
- 1 packet (2 and 1/4 tsp) instant yeast
- 1/4 cup (60g) butter, melted
- 1 cup (240ml) warm milk

Instructions:

1. **Prepare dough**: Combine flour, cheese, garlic powder, salt, yeast, milk, and butter. Knead until smooth.
2. **First rise**: Cover and let rise for 1 hour.
3. **Shape rolls**: Divide into balls and arrange in a greased pan.
4. **Second rise**: Let rise for 30 minutes.
5. **Bake**: Bake at 375°F (190°C) for 18-20 minutes.

Rosemary Sea Salt Rolls

Ingredients:

- 3 and 1/2 cups (420g) all-purpose flour
- 1 teaspoon salt
- 1 tablespoon fresh rosemary, chopped
- 1/4 cup (60ml) olive oil
- 1 cup (240ml) warm water
- 1 packet (2 and 1/4 tsp) instant yeast

Instructions:

1. **Mix ingredients**: Combine flour, salt, rosemary, yeast, water, and olive oil. Knead until smooth.
2. **First rise**: Let rise for 1 hour.
3. **Shape rolls**: Form into balls and place on a baking sheet.
4. **Second rise**: Let rise for 30 minutes.
5. **Bake**: Brush with olive oil, sprinkle sea salt, and bake at 375°F (190°C) for 15-18 minutes.

Soft Pretzel Rolls

Ingredients:

- 4 cups (480g) bread flour
- 2 teaspoons salt
- 1 tablespoon sugar
- 1 packet (2 and 1/4 tsp) instant yeast
- 1 cup (240ml) warm water
- 1/4 cup (60g) unsalted butter, melted
- 1/4 cup (60g) baking soda (for water bath)

Instructions:

1. **Make dough**: Combine flour, salt, sugar, yeast, water, and butter. Knead until smooth.
2. **First rise**: Let rise for 1 hour.
3. **Shape rolls**: Form balls and boil in a baking soda water bath for 30 seconds.
4. **Bake**: Sprinkle with coarse salt and bake at 400°F (200°C) for 15-18 minutes.

Sweet Cornbread Rolls

Ingredients:

- 2 cups (240g) all-purpose flour
- 1 cup (120g) cornmeal
- 1/4 cup (50g) sugar
- 1 teaspoon salt
- 1 packet (2 and 1/4 tsp) instant yeast
- 1 cup (240ml) warm milk
- 1/4 cup (60g) butter, melted

Instructions:

1. **Mix dough**: Combine flour, cornmeal, sugar, salt, yeast, milk, and butter. Knead until smooth.
2. **First rise**: Cover and let rise for 1 hour.
3. **Shape rolls**: Form into balls and place in a greased baking dish.
4. **Bake**: Bake at 375°F (190°C) for 15-20 minutes.

Sesame Seed Rolls

Ingredients:

- 4 cups (480g) all-purpose flour
- 1/4 cup (50g) sugar
- 1 teaspoon salt
- 1 packet (2 and 1/4 tsp) instant yeast
- 1 cup (240ml) warm water
- 1/4 cup (60ml) olive oil
- 2 tablespoons sesame seeds

Instructions:

1. **Combine ingredients**: Mix flour, sugar, salt, yeast, water, and oil. Knead until smooth.
2. **First rise**: Let rise for 1 hour.
3. **Shape rolls**: Form into balls and top with sesame seeds.
4. **Bake**: Bake at 375°F (190°C) for 15-18 minutes.

Poppy Seed Rolls

Ingredients:

- 3 and 1/2 cups (420g) all-purpose flour
- 1 teaspoon salt
- 1/4 cup (50g) sugar
- 1 packet (2 and 1/4 tsp) instant yeast
- 1 cup (240ml) warm milk
- 1/4 cup (60g) butter, melted
- 2 tablespoons poppy seeds

Instructions:

1. **Mix dough**: Combine flour, salt, sugar, yeast, milk, and butter. Knead until smooth.
2. **First rise**: Let rise for 1 hour.
3. **Shape rolls**: Form balls and sprinkle with poppy seeds.
4. **Bake**: Bake at 375°F (190°C) for 15-20 minutes.

Cinnamon Honey Rolls

Ingredients:

- 3 cups (360g) all-purpose flour
- 1/4 cup (50g) sugar
- 1 teaspoon salt
- 1 packet (2 and 1/4 tsp) instant yeast
- 1 cup (240ml) warm milk
- 1/4 cup (60g) butter, melted
- 1 teaspoon cinnamon
- 2 tablespoons honey

Instructions:

1. **Combine dough**: Mix flour, sugar, salt, yeast, cinnamon, milk, and butter. Knead until smooth.
2. **First rise**: Let rise for 1 hour.
3. **Shape rolls**: Form into balls and drizzle with honey.
4. **Bake**: Bake at 375°F (190°C) for 15-18 minutes.

Cheddar Jalapeño Rolls

Ingredients:

- 4 cups (480g) all-purpose flour
- 1 packet (2 and 1/4 tsp) instant yeast
- 1 teaspoon salt
- 1 tablespoon sugar
- 1/2 cup (120ml) warm milk
- 1/4 cup (60g) melted butter
- 1 large egg
- 1 cup (100g) shredded cheddar cheese
- 2-3 jalapeños, finely chopped

Instructions:

1. **Mix dough**: Combine flour, yeast, salt, sugar, milk, butter, and egg. Knead until smooth.
2. **Add cheese and jalapeños**: Gently fold in the cheddar cheese and jalapeños.
3. **First rise**: Cover and let rise for 1 hour.
4. **Shape rolls**: Form dough into rolls and place in a greased baking dish.
5. **Second rise**: Let rise for 30 minutes.
6. **Bake**: Bake at 375°F (190°C) for 15-20 minutes.

Olive Oil and Herb Rolls

Ingredients:

- 3 and 1/2 cups (420g) all-purpose flour
- 1 packet (2 and 1/4 tsp) instant yeast
- 1 teaspoon salt
- 1 teaspoon dried thyme
- 1 teaspoon dried rosemary
- 1/4 cup (60ml) olive oil
- 1 cup (240ml) warm water

Instructions:

1. **Mix dough**: Combine flour, yeast, salt, thyme, rosemary, olive oil, and warm water. Knead until smooth.
2. **First rise**: Cover and let rise for 1 hour.
3. **Shape rolls**: Divide the dough into small balls and place them on a baking sheet.
4. **Second rise**: Let rise for 30 minutes.
5. **Bake**: Bake at 375°F (190°C) for 15-18 minutes.

Maple Butter Rolls

Ingredients:

- 4 cups (480g) all-purpose flour
- 1 packet (2 and 1/4 tsp) instant yeast
- 1 teaspoon salt
- 1/4 cup (60g) sugar
- 1/2 cup (120ml) warm milk
- 1/4 cup (60g) melted butter
- 1/4 cup (60ml) maple syrup

Instructions:

1. **Combine dough**: Mix flour, yeast, salt, sugar, milk, butter, and maple syrup. Knead until smooth.
2. **First rise**: Let rise for 1 hour.
3. **Shape rolls**: Divide the dough into rolls and arrange them in a greased baking pan.
4. **Second rise**: Let rise for 30 minutes.
5. **Bake**: Bake at 375°F (190°C) for 15-18 minutes.

Rye Dinner Rolls

Ingredients:

- 2 cups (240g) all-purpose flour
- 2 cups (240g) rye flour
- 1 packet (2 and 1/4 tsp) instant yeast
- 1 teaspoon salt
- 1 tablespoon sugar
- 1 cup (240ml) warm water
- 2 tablespoons butter, melted

Instructions:

1. **Combine dry ingredients**: Mix both flours, yeast, salt, and sugar.
2. **Add wet ingredients**: Gradually add warm water and melted butter. Knead until smooth.
3. **First rise**: Let rise for 1 hour.
4. **Shape rolls**: Shape dough into rolls and place on a greased baking sheet.
5. **Second rise**: Let rise for 30 minutes.
6. **Bake**: Bake at 375°F (190°C) for 15-20 minutes.

Multigrain Rolls

Ingredients:

- 3 cups (360g) all-purpose flour
- 1 cup (120g) multigrain flour (or a mix of oats, barley, etc.)
- 1 packet (2 and 1/4 tsp) instant yeast
- 1 teaspoon salt
- 2 tablespoons honey
- 1 cup (240ml) warm water
- 2 tablespoons olive oil

Instructions:

1. **Mix dough**: Combine all-purpose flour, multigrain flour, yeast, salt, honey, warm water, and olive oil. Knead until smooth.
2. **First rise**: Let rise for 1 hour.
3. **Shape rolls**: Shape dough into small balls and arrange them on a baking sheet.
4. **Second rise**: Let rise for 30 minutes.
5. **Bake**: Bake at 375°F (190°C) for 15-18 minutes.

Sun-Dried Tomato Basil Rolls

Ingredients:

- 3 and 1/2 cups (420g) all-purpose flour
- 1 packet (2 and 1/4 tsp) instant yeast
- 1 teaspoon salt
- 1 tablespoon olive oil
- 1/2 cup (120ml) warm water
- 1/4 cup (50g) sun-dried tomatoes, chopped
- 2 tablespoons fresh basil, chopped

Instructions:

1. **Mix dough**: Combine flour, yeast, salt, olive oil, and warm water. Knead until smooth.
2. **Add tomatoes and basil**: Fold in the sun-dried tomatoes and basil.
3. **First rise**: Let rise for 1 hour.
4. **Shape rolls**: Form dough into small rolls and place them on a greased baking sheet.
5. **Second rise**: Let rise for 30 minutes.
6. **Bake**: Bake at 375°F (190°C) for 15-18 minutes.

Asiago Cheese Rolls

Ingredients:

- 3 cups (360g) all-purpose flour
- 1 packet (2 and 1/4 tsp) instant yeast
- 1 teaspoon salt
- 1/2 teaspoon garlic powder
- 1 cup (100g) shredded Asiago cheese
- 1/4 cup (60ml) olive oil
- 1 cup (240ml) warm water

Instructions:

1. **Mix dough**: Combine flour, yeast, salt, garlic powder, cheese, olive oil, and warm water. Knead until smooth.
2. **First rise**: Let rise for 1 hour.
3. **Shape rolls**: Form dough into rolls and place on a greased baking sheet.
4. **Second rise**: Let rise for 30 minutes.
5. **Bake**: Bake at 375°F (190°C) for 15-20 minutes.

Dill and Cheddar Rolls

Ingredients:

- 3 cups (360g) all-purpose flour
- 1 packet (2 and 1/4 tsp) instant yeast
- 1 teaspoon salt
- 1 cup (100g) shredded cheddar cheese
- 1 tablespoon fresh dill, chopped
- 1 cup (240ml) warm water
- 2 tablespoons butter, melted

Instructions:

1. **Mix dough**: Combine flour, yeast, salt, cheese, dill, warm water, and butter. Knead until smooth.
2. **First rise**: Let rise for 1 hour.
3. **Shape rolls**: Shape dough into rolls and place them on a baking sheet.
4. **Second rise**: Let rise for 30 minutes.
5. **Bake**: Bake at 375°F (190°C) for 15-18 minutes.

Caramelized Onion Rolls

Ingredients:

- 3 cups (360g) all-purpose flour
- 1 packet (2 and 1/4 tsp) instant yeast
- 1 teaspoon salt
- 1 cup (240ml) warm water
- 2 tablespoons olive oil
- 1 large onion, caramelized
- 2 tablespoons fresh thyme, chopped

Instructions:

1. **Prepare caramelized onions**: In a skillet, cook onions in olive oil over medium-low heat until golden and soft.
2. **Mix dough**: Combine flour, yeast, salt, warm water, and olive oil. Knead until smooth.
3. **Add onions and thyme**: Mix in caramelized onions and thyme.
4. **First rise**: Let rise for 1 hour.
5. **Shape rolls**: Divide dough into rolls and place on a greased baking sheet.
6. **Second rise**: Let rise for 30 minutes.
7. **Bake**: Bake at 375°F (190°C) for 15-20 minutes.

Lemon Thyme Rolls

Ingredients:

- 3 and 1/2 cups (420g) all-purpose flour
- 1 packet (2 and 1/4 tsp) instant yeast
- 1 teaspoon salt
- 1 tablespoon fresh thyme, chopped
- Zest of 1 lemon
- 1/2 cup (120ml) warm milk
- 2 tablespoons butter, melted

Instructions:

1. **Mix dough**: Combine flour, yeast, salt, thyme, lemon zest, milk, and butter. Knead until smooth.
2. **First rise**: Let rise for 1 hour.
3. **Shape rolls**: Form dough into rolls and arrange them on a greased baking sheet.
4. **Second rise**: Let rise for 30 minutes.
5. **Bake**: Bake at 375°F (190°C) for 15-18 minutes.

Spelt Flour Rolls

Ingredients:

- 2 cups (240g) spelt flour
- 1 and 1/2 cups (180g) all-purpose flour
- 1 packet (2 and 1/4 tsp) instant yeast
- 1 teaspoon salt
- 1 tablespoon honey
- 1 cup (240ml) warm water
- 2 tablespoons olive oil

Instructions:

1. **Combine dry ingredients**: In a large bowl, mix spelt flour, all-purpose flour, yeast, and salt.
2. **Add wet ingredients**: Add honey, warm water, and olive oil. Knead until smooth.
3. **First rise**: Let the dough rise for 1 hour, covered.
4. **Shape rolls**: Divide dough into rolls and place them on a greased baking sheet.
5. **Second rise**: Let the dough rise for another 30 minutes.
6. **Bake**: Bake at 375°F (190°C) for 15-20 minutes, until golden.

Crusty French Rolls

Ingredients:

- 4 cups (480g) all-purpose flour
- 1 packet (2 and 1/4 tsp) instant yeast
- 1 teaspoon salt
- 1 tablespoon sugar
- 1 cup (240ml) warm water
- 2 tablespoons olive oil

Instructions:

1. **Mix dough**: In a large bowl, combine flour, yeast, salt, and sugar. Add warm water and olive oil, kneading until smooth.
2. **First rise**: Let rise for 1 hour, covered with a towel.
3. **Shape rolls**: Divide dough into 8 equal portions, shaping each into a round roll.
4. **Second rise**: Let rise for another 30 minutes.
5. **Bake**: Bake at 400°F (200°C) for 18-20 minutes, until crusty and golden.
6. **Cool**: Cool on a wire rack.

Pumpkin Spice Rolls

Ingredients:

- 3 cups (360g) all-purpose flour
- 1 packet (2 and 1/4 tsp) instant yeast
- 1 teaspoon salt
- 1 teaspoon ground cinnamon
- 1/2 teaspoon ground nutmeg
- 1/4 teaspoon ground ginger
- 1 cup (240g) canned pumpkin
- 1/4 cup (60g) sugar
- 1/2 cup (120ml) warm milk
- 1/4 cup (60g) butter, melted
- 1 egg

Instructions:

1. **Combine dry ingredients**: Mix flour, yeast, salt, cinnamon, nutmeg, and ginger in a bowl.
2. **Add wet ingredients**: Combine pumpkin, sugar, warm milk, butter, and egg. Stir into the dry ingredients, kneading until smooth.
3. **First rise**: Let dough rise for 1 hour.
4. **Shape rolls**: Shape dough into small balls and place in a greased pan.
5. **Second rise**: Let rise for another 30 minutes.
6. **Bake**: Bake at 375°F (190°C) for 15-18 minutes.

Orange Honey Butter Rolls

Ingredients:

- 4 cups (480g) all-purpose flour
- 1 packet (2 and 1/4 tsp) instant yeast
- 1 teaspoon salt
- 2 tablespoons honey
- Zest of 1 orange
- 1/2 cup (120ml) warm milk
- 1/4 cup (60g) butter, melted
- 1/4 cup (60ml) fresh orange juice

Instructions:

1. **Combine dough**: Mix flour, yeast, salt, honey, orange zest, warm milk, butter, and orange juice in a bowl. Knead until smooth.
2. **First rise**: Let the dough rise for 1 hour.
3. **Shape rolls**: Shape dough into rolls and place on a greased baking sheet.
4. **Second rise**: Let the dough rise for another 30 minutes.
5. **Bake**: Bake at 375°F (190°C) for 15-20 minutes.

Cranberry Walnut Rolls

Ingredients:

- 3 cups (360g) all-purpose flour
- 1 packet (2 and 1/4 tsp) instant yeast
- 1 teaspoon salt
- 1/2 cup (50g) dried cranberries
- 1/2 cup (50g) walnuts, chopped
- 1 tablespoon sugar
- 1 cup (240ml) warm water
- 2 tablespoons olive oil

Instructions:

1. **Mix dough**: Combine flour, yeast, salt, sugar, warm water, and olive oil. Knead until smooth.
2. **Add cranberries and walnuts**: Fold in cranberries and walnuts.
3. **First rise**: Let rise for 1 hour.
4. **Shape rolls**: Shape dough into rolls and place on a greased baking sheet.
5. **Second rise**: Let rise for 30 minutes.
6. **Bake**: Bake at 375°F (190°C) for 15-18 minutes.

Bacon and Cheddar Rolls

Ingredients:

- 3 cups (360g) all-purpose flour
- 1 packet (2 and 1/4 tsp) instant yeast
- 1 teaspoon salt
- 1 cup (100g) cheddar cheese, shredded
- 1/2 cup (50g) cooked bacon, crumbled
- 1 tablespoon sugar
- 1 cup (240ml) warm water
- 2 tablespoons butter, melted

Instructions:

1. **Mix dough**: Combine flour, yeast, salt, sugar, warm water, and melted butter. Knead until smooth.
2. **Add bacon and cheese**: Fold in cheddar and crumbled bacon.
3. **First rise**: Let rise for 1 hour.
4. **Shape rolls**: Divide dough into small portions and place in a greased pan.
5. **Second rise**: Let rise for another 30 minutes.
6. **Bake**: Bake at 375°F (190°C) for 15-18 minutes.

Herb and Garlic Knots

Ingredients:

- 3 cups (360g) all-purpose flour
- 1 packet (2 and 1/4 tsp) instant yeast
- 1 teaspoon salt
- 2 tablespoons olive oil
- 1 cup (240ml) warm water
- 2 tablespoons garlic, minced
- 1 tablespoon fresh parsley, chopped

Instructions:

1. **Prepare dough**: Combine flour, yeast, salt, olive oil, and warm water. Knead until smooth.
2. **First rise**: Let dough rise for 1 hour.
3. **Shape knots**: Shape dough into small pieces and tie them into knots.
4. **Garlic butter**: In a bowl, mix melted butter, garlic, and parsley. Brush over each knot.
5. **Second rise**: Let rise for 30 minutes.
6. **Bake**: Bake at 375°F (190°C) for 15-20 minutes.

Ricotta Rolls

Ingredients:

- 3 cups (360g) all-purpose flour
- 1 packet (2 and 1/4 tsp) instant yeast
- 1 teaspoon salt
- 1 cup (240g) ricotta cheese
- 1/4 cup (60g) sugar
- 1/2 cup (120ml) warm milk
- 2 tablespoons butter, melted

Instructions:

1. **Mix dough**: Combine flour, yeast, salt, ricotta, sugar, warm milk, and melted butter. Knead until smooth.
2. **First rise**: Let rise for 1 hour.
3. **Shape rolls**: Form dough into rolls and place on a greased baking sheet.
4. **Second rise**: Let rise for 30 minutes.
5. **Bake**: Bake at 375°F (190°C) for 15-18 minutes.

Black Pepper and Parmesan Rolls

Ingredients:

- 3 cups (360g) all-purpose flour
- 1 packet (2 and 1/4 tsp) instant yeast
- 1 teaspoon salt
- 1/2 teaspoon ground black pepper
- 1/2 cup (50g) grated Parmesan cheese
- 1 cup (240ml) warm water
- 2 tablespoons olive oil

Instructions:

1. **Combine dough**: Mix flour, yeast, salt, black pepper, warm water, and olive oil. Knead until smooth.
2. **Add Parmesan**: Fold in grated Parmesan cheese.
3. **First rise**: Let rise for 1 hour.
4. **Shape rolls**: Divide dough into rolls and place them on a greased baking sheet.
5. **Second rise**: Let rise for 30 minutes.
6. **Bake**: Bake at 375°F (190°C) for 15-20 minutes.

Cinnamon Raisin Rolls

Ingredients:

- 3 cups (360g) all-purpose flour
- 1 packet (2 and 1/4 tsp) instant yeast
- 1 teaspoon salt
- 1/4 cup (50g) sugar
- 1/2 cup (120ml) warm milk
- 1/4 cup (60g) butter, melted
- 1 egg
- 1 cup (150g) raisins
- 2 teaspoons ground cinnamon

Instructions:

1. **Prepare dough**: In a bowl, combine flour, yeast, salt, and sugar. Add warm milk, melted butter, and egg. Knead until smooth.
2. **First rise**: Let dough rise for 1 hour, covered.
3. **Shape rolls**: Roll dough into a rectangle, spread cinnamon, and sprinkle raisins on top. Roll up tightly and slice into rolls.
4. **Second rise**: Let rolls rise for 30 minutes.
5. **Bake**: Bake at 375°F (190°C) for 18-20 minutes until golden.

Spinach and Feta Rolls

Ingredients:

- 3 cups (360g) all-purpose flour
- 1 packet (2 and 1/4 tsp) instant yeast
- 1 teaspoon salt
- 1 cup (240ml) warm water
- 2 tablespoons olive oil
- 1 cup (150g) fresh spinach, chopped
- 1/2 cup (75g) feta cheese, crumbled
- 1 tablespoon garlic, minced

Instructions:

1. **Mix dough**: Combine flour, yeast, salt, warm water, and olive oil. Knead until smooth.
2. **First rise**: Let dough rise for 1 hour.
3. **Prepare filling**: Sauté spinach and garlic in olive oil until wilted. Let cool, then mix with crumbled feta.
4. **Shape rolls**: Roll dough out, spread spinach mixture, and roll up. Slice into rolls.
5. **Second rise**: Let rise for 30 minutes.
6. **Bake**: Bake at 375°F (190°C) for 18-20 minutes.

Sweet Potato Rolls

Ingredients:

- 2 cups (240g) all-purpose flour
- 1 packet (2 and 1/4 tsp) instant yeast
- 1 teaspoon salt
- 1 cup (240g) mashed sweet potato
- 1/4 cup (50g) brown sugar
- 1/4 cup (60ml) warm milk
- 1/4 cup (60g) butter, melted

Instructions:

1. **Prepare dough**: Mix flour, yeast, salt, mashed sweet potato, brown sugar, warm milk, and melted butter. Knead until smooth.
2. **First rise**: Let dough rise for 1 hour.
3. **Shape rolls**: Shape dough into small balls and place on a greased baking sheet.
4. **Second rise**: Let rise for 30 minutes.
5. **Bake**: Bake at 375°F (190°C) for 15-18 minutes until golden.

Yeast-Free Dinner Rolls

Ingredients:

- 2 cups (240g) all-purpose flour
- 1 tablespoon baking powder
- 1 teaspoon salt
- 1/2 cup (120ml) milk
- 1/4 cup (60g) butter, softened
- 1 tablespoon honey

Instructions:

1. **Mix dry ingredients**: In a bowl, combine flour, baking powder, and salt.
2. **Add wet ingredients**: Add milk, softened butter, and honey. Stir until dough comes together.
3. **Shape rolls**: Shape dough into small balls and place on a greased baking sheet.
4. **Bake**: Bake at 375°F (190°C) for 12-15 minutes until golden.

Vegan Herb Rolls

Ingredients:

- 3 cups (360g) all-purpose flour
- 1 packet (2 and 1/4 tsp) instant yeast
- 1 teaspoon salt
- 1 tablespoon olive oil
- 1 cup (240ml) warm water
- 2 tablespoons fresh herbs (parsley, thyme, rosemary), chopped
- 1 tablespoon sugar

Instructions:

1. **Mix dough**: Combine flour, yeast, salt, fresh herbs, sugar, and warm water. Knead until smooth.
2. **First rise**: Let dough rise for 1 hour.
3. **Shape rolls**: Shape dough into small rolls and place on a greased baking sheet.
4. **Second rise**: Let rise for 30 minutes.
5. **Bake**: Bake at 375°F (190°C) for 15-18 minutes until golden.

Gluten-Free Dinner Rolls

Ingredients:

- 2 cups (240g) gluten-free all-purpose flour
- 1 packet (2 and 1/4 tsp) instant yeast
- 1 teaspoon salt
- 1 tablespoon sugar
- 1 cup (240ml) warm water
- 1/4 cup (60g) olive oil
- 1 egg (or flax egg for vegan option)

Instructions:

1. **Mix dough**: Combine gluten-free flour, yeast, salt, sugar, warm water, olive oil, and egg. Stir to form dough.
2. **First rise**: Let dough rise for 1 hour, covered.
3. **Shape rolls**: Spoon dough into greased muffin tins or shape into rolls.
4. **Second rise**: Let rise for 30 minutes.
5. **Bake**: Bake at 375°F (190°C) for 18-20 minutes.

Chive and Sour Cream Rolls

Ingredients:

- 3 cups (360g) all-purpose flour
- 1 packet (2 and 1/4 tsp) instant yeast
- 1 teaspoon salt
- 1/4 cup (60g) sour cream
- 1/2 cup (120ml) warm water
- 2 tablespoons butter, melted
- 1/4 cup (30g) fresh chives, chopped
- 1 tablespoon sugar

Instructions:

1. **Mix dough**: In a bowl, combine flour, yeast, salt, sugar, and chopped chives.
2. **Add wet ingredients**: Mix in sour cream, warm water, and melted butter. Knead the dough until smooth.
3. **First rise**: Let dough rise for 1 hour or until doubled in size.
4. **Shape rolls**: Shape dough into small rolls and place on a greased baking sheet.
5. **Second rise**: Let rise for 30 minutes.
6. **Bake**: Bake at 375°F (190°C) for 15-18 minutes until golden brown.

Molasses Wheat Rolls

Ingredients:

- 2 cups (240g) whole wheat flour
- 1 cup (120g) all-purpose flour
- 1 packet (2 and 1/4 tsp) instant yeast
- 1 teaspoon salt
- 1 tablespoon molasses
- 1/4 cup (60ml) warm water
- 1/4 cup (60g) butter, softened
- 1/4 cup (60ml) milk
- 1 tablespoon honey

Instructions:

1. **Mix dry ingredients**: In a large bowl, combine whole wheat flour, all-purpose flour, yeast, and salt.
2. **Add wet ingredients**: In another bowl, whisk together molasses, warm water, butter, milk, and honey.
3. **Combine**: Gradually add wet ingredients to dry ingredients and knead until smooth.
4. **First rise**: Let dough rise for 1 hour, covered.
5. **Shape rolls**: Shape dough into small rolls and place on a greased baking sheet.
6. **Second rise**: Let rise for 30 minutes.
7. **Bake**: Bake at 375°F (190°C) for 18-20 minutes.

Buttery Crescent Rolls

Ingredients:

- 2 cups (240g) all-purpose flour
- 1 packet (2 and 1/4 tsp) instant yeast
- 1 teaspoon salt
- 1/4 cup (60g) butter, softened
- 1/2 cup (120ml) warm milk
- 1 tablespoon sugar
- 1 egg, beaten

Instructions:

1. **Mix dough**: In a bowl, combine flour, yeast, salt, and sugar. Add in warm milk and softened butter. Stir until dough forms.
2. **Knead**: Knead dough for 8-10 minutes until smooth.
3. **First rise**: Let dough rise for 1 hour.
4. **Shape rolls**: Roll dough out into a circle, then cut into wedges. Roll each wedge into a crescent shape.
5. **Second rise**: Let rise for 30 minutes.
6. **Bake**: Brush rolls with beaten egg, then bake at 375°F (190°C) for 15-18 minutes until golden.

Pesto Swirl Rolls

Ingredients:

- 3 cups (360g) all-purpose flour
- 1 packet (2 and 1/4 tsp) instant yeast
- 1 teaspoon salt
- 1/4 cup (60ml) olive oil
- 1/2 cup (120ml) warm milk
- 1/4 cup (60g) pesto sauce (store-bought or homemade)
- 1 tablespoon sugar

Instructions:

1. **Mix dough**: Combine flour, yeast, salt, and sugar in a bowl. Add warm milk and olive oil. Knead until smooth.
2. **First rise**: Let dough rise for 1 hour, covered.
3. **Prepare filling**: Roll dough into a rectangle and spread pesto sauce evenly.
4. **Shape rolls**: Roll up dough into a log, then slice into rolls.
5. **Second rise**: Let rise for 30 minutes.
6. **Bake**: Bake at 375°F (190°C) for 18-20 minutes.

Lemon Poppy Seed Rolls

Ingredients:

- 2 cups (240g) all-purpose flour
- 1 packet (2 and 1/4 tsp) instant yeast
- 1 teaspoon salt
- 1/4 cup (60ml) lemon juice
- 1/2 cup (120ml) warm milk
- 1 tablespoon sugar
- 2 tablespoons poppy seeds
- 1/4 cup (60g) butter, melted

Instructions:

1. **Mix dough**: In a bowl, combine flour, yeast, salt, sugar, and poppy seeds.
2. **Add wet ingredients**: Pour in warm milk and lemon juice. Knead until smooth.
3. **First rise**: Let dough rise for 1 hour.
4. **Shape rolls**: Shape dough into small rolls and place on a greased baking sheet.
5. **Second rise**: Let rise for 30 minutes.
6. **Bake**: Bake at 375°F (190°C) for 15-18 minutes.

Flaky Butter Layer Rolls

Ingredients:

- 2 cups (240g) all-purpose flour
- 1 packet (2 and 1/4 tsp) instant yeast
- 1 teaspoon salt
- 1/2 cup (120g) cold butter, cut into cubes
- 1/2 cup (120ml) warm milk
- 1 tablespoon sugar

Instructions:

1. **Mix dry ingredients**: Combine flour, yeast, salt, and sugar in a large bowl.
2. **Cut in butter**: Add cold butter cubes to the flour mixture and cut in using a pastry cutter or your fingers until the mixture resembles coarse crumbs.
3. **Add milk**: Gradually add warm milk and stir until dough comes together.
4. **First rise**: Let dough rise for 1 hour.
5. **Shape rolls**: Roll dough out and fold it into layers. Cut into rolls and place on a greased baking sheet.
6. **Second rise**: Let rise for 30 minutes.
7. **Bake**: Bake at 375°F (190°C) for 18-20 minutes.

Almond Milk Dinner Rolls

Ingredients:

- 3 cups (360g) all-purpose flour
- 1 packet (2 and 1/4 tsp) instant yeast
- 1 teaspoon salt
- 1/4 cup (60ml) almond milk
- 1/4 cup (60g) butter, softened
- 1 tablespoon sugar
- 1 egg

Instructions:

1. **Mix dough**: Combine flour, yeast, salt, and sugar in a bowl. Add almond milk, butter, and egg. Knead until smooth.
2. **First rise**: Let dough rise for 1 hour.
3. **Shape rolls**: Shape dough into small balls and place on a greased baking sheet.
4. **Second rise**: Let rise for 30 minutes.
5. **Bake**: Bake at 375°F (190°C) for 15-18 minutes.

www.ingramcontent.com/pod-product-compliance
Lightning Source LLC
LaVergne TN
LVHW081459060526
838201LV00056BA/2838